REAL ESTATE INVESTING FOR OUR CHILDREN

A Road Map for Generational Wealth

Written by
Munashe Joel Masuka

Author Biography

Munashe Joel Masuka is the author of the book titled Real Estate Investing for Our Children (2020). He graduated from Trent University with an honors degree in Biochemistry and Molecular Biology and is also a Power Engineer.

Munashe enjoys researching anything that has to do with real estate investing and creating generational wealth. In 2019, he used his knowledge of real estate to help a syndication group fully analyze the risks and rewards of a recent real estate accusation. As a real estate owner and investor, his goal is to help others achieve generational wealth through real estate investing. The two times in his life where he found himself homeless has been a primary motivator behind his drive and love for real estate and remains so to this day.

Originally born in Africa, Munashe moved to the United States when he was nine years old. Two years after graduating from high school, he moved to Canada, where he currently resides.

Today, Munashe is a loving father and husband who enjoys working out, snorkeling, and going on vacations with his family in his free time.

Acknowledgments

Firstly, I would like to thank God for giving me the opportunity to write this book and the determination to see its creation through.

I would also like to thank my parents, Joel and Josephine Masuka, for all the sacrifices they made for us and every opportunity they gave us. They are both the true definition of what great parents are.

I would also like to thank my wife and fellow real estate investor, Ruvimbo Masuka. Thank you for all your moral support during this real estate journey. We make a great real estate team, and I couldn't have done the things we did without you.

I also want to take this time to thank my little brother Eldridge Masuka, a commercial real estate assessor. Thank you for all the information you gave me for this book and for introducing me to the real estate game.

Thank you so much, Tsitsi (Nurse) and Donald Tavuma (certified accountant), for your moral support and helping me with the real estate strategy we currently have in place.

Thank you so much to Davison and Claris Ruwende, CA chartered accountants and fellow real estate investors, for giving me information on the accounting side of things, specifically regarding real estate and general investments.

Thank you Takudzwa Chinyani, real estate investor, for always supporting my ideas and for helping with the real estate game plan.

I also want to thank Peter Woldu, real estate agent and investor, for helping us get our property. He went above and beyond with all the information he provided for us.

Big thanks to the Tariro Visions INC, a syndication group, for showing me that with dedication and the right group of people, it is possible to start a real estate business.

Thank you to Marcelo Luz, a commercial real estate and residential investor, for all your advice and tips in regards to commercial real estate, how to structure your real estate business and showing me how to select the correct property manager when we rented out our first property.

Thank you to Mbongeni Mtetwa, a graphic design expert, for all your help designing the book cover.

Last, but most definitely not least, I want to thank Jayden Masuka and my future children for sparking this fire under me to be a great father.

Table of Contents

CHAPTER 1

The Importance of Intergenerational Wealth

Dear children, by the time you read this book, I am sure you will have heard someone mention the phrase intergenerational or generational wealth around you at some point. You might have even watched a movie, listened to a song, or found something on the internet that talks about it. Even the Bible tells us about generational wealth in proverbs 13:22, which states that "A good person leaves an inheritance for their children's children and the wealth of a sinner is stored up for the righteous."

Intergenerational wealth can be defined as money, businesses, knowledge, or any asset passed down from one generation to another. This chapter will demonstrate why generational wealth is important and why there is a big wealth gap between minorities and people of European descent in North America.

One of the reasons why generational wealth is important is that most wealthy people don't get wealthy within one lifetime. Although there are exceptions, many people become wealthy because someone in their family left them with what I would call a head start in life. This head start can come in the form of a business, money (most of the time it's from life insurance), or some other type of asset that's been passed down. This head start helps their family financially, which then, in turn, helps to give them more options in life.

To put things in perspective, imagine two people on a track about to run 100 yards. At the end of the 100 yards, they will gain financial freedom (each yard being equal to one year). These two people happen to be identical twins with the same build, strength, and stamina. One of the twins is called Sam and the other Jonathan. Now, imagine right before the race starts, Sam has moved 50 yards ahead of Jonathan. This means that Sam only has to run 50 yards to get to the 100-yard mark in order to gain financial freedom. On the other hand, Jonathan still has to run the full 100 yards to gain financial freedom.

In terms of years, Sam will be financially free when he is 50 years old and Jonathan at 100 years old. For Jonathan to finish the race at the same time as Sam, he will have to work twice as hard as Jonathan to get the same finishing time as him. Remember that they are twins and have the same build, stamina, and strength. Given Sam's advantage, this means it's going to be almost impossible for Jonathan to achieve financial freedom at the same time as Sam. Furthermore, Jonathan might not even achieve financial freedom in his lifetime at all.

That is what generational wealth does to people's lives; it gives them a head start in life financially. The next generation's responsibility will be to properly manage the assets, businesses, or money handed down to them so that the following generation has more than what they started with. As long as each generation continues to grow the assets, businesses, or money, then each generation that follows after will become wealthier. Eventually, instead of starting at the 50-yard mark, the upcoming generation will start at the 40-yard line. The generation after them will start at the 30-yard line. Until eventually, a generation will be born already at the 100-yard mark.

One of the reasons why there is a significant wealth gap between minorities and people of European descent is that most European descendants have been given a substantial financial head start in life. Before the slave trade was abolished, European ancestors used slavery to build their wealth, and current systems like systemic racism are put in place to help them continue to build their wealth. They made sure that minorities had next to nothing, while the Europeans continued to build their wealth, farms, and other businesses on the backs of the enslaved minorities. Not only did they pass down their farms and businesses to their children, but also passed down their racist mindset. For multiple generations, minorities had next to nothing to pass down to their children because of this cycle. While, simultaneously, European descendants saw their wealth compound generation after generation.

Even after slavery was abolished, Europeans put systems in place to ensure that they continued to gain wealth while ensuring that minorities remained poor and oppressed. It is as if minorities were finally allowed to play the monopoly game after slavery was abolished, but the game had been ongoing for hundreds of years before their inclusion.

Minorities had missed multiple turns to play. They had been stuck in jail for centuries due to the systems put in place to keep them there. Unfortunately, by the time minorities had a chance to roll the dice and play, all the properties were owned except one or two of the cheapest ones. All minorities can do at this point in the monopoly game is to hope that little money they have is enough to at least go around once, and maybe, just maybe, they will have the chance to buy one of the cheap properties that are still available.

An example of a real-life system implemented and executed by individuals of European descent that enforced housing discrimination was known as redlining. Redlining was a legal and government-endorsed program that would deny mortgages and homeownership opportunities to African Americans and other minorities. Even though redlining is now illegal, the mindset has been passed down to today's generations.

Some people of European descent and other races don't like it when minorities move into their neighborhoods. This is because of the systems implemented to lower the property values in areas where there is a significant population of minorities. On the other hand, this same system will increase the property values in regions without a minority presence. People of European descent may be accepting of a few minorities to move in, but when a large number of minority families start moving in, they tend to see that as a threat to their property value.

Gentrification is another system that allows those with money to take over and systematically kick out impoverished communities in a particular area that they were living within. Keep in mind that the majority of people with money had it passed down to them. They do this for many reasons, but the major one is that they are often speculating that the area that the poor individuals are currently living in could be profitable in the future.

According to an article written by Stephen Miller in 2020, minorities get paid less than Europeans for the same job, even though they have the same educational background. On the subject of education, schools in areas with a large number of minorities tend to be less funded and are given fewer resources than those without minorities. This is mostly because property taxes are used to fund the school's expenses in that specific school district. So, if you live in an area where the property value for a single-family home is high, then the schools around that area will be adequately funded.

On the other hand, if you live in an area where property values are low, then the schools in that district have a higher probability of being underfunded. It is yet another system put into our government to keep minorities less educated and poor but, on the other hand, educate and enrich the European descendants.

I won't even get into the criminal systems put in place to oppress minority groups, but I just wanted to give you a small picture of how minorities have been set up to fail within the current systems that are in place today. Hopefully, things will change drastically by the time you read this book. There are many other systems out there. Some that we might not even be aware of, but those are stories for another book. We must not lose focus on this book's intention, which is to teach you how to use real estate to build generational wealth.

Another reason why intergenerational wealth is important is that it gives us parents peace of mind. The last thing any parent with a good heart wants to do is leave their child in poverty or in a worse situation than the one they grew up in themselves. Any good-hearted parent wants to see their child excel and succeed in whatever they want to do. Most parents will do whatever it takes to help their children succeed. Unfortunately, when it comes to minority families, the lack of financial education makes it difficult to set up children for financial success. Other factors come into play, like the people around you, racism, and the opportunities available to you, but one of the most important is the lack of education. There is a lack of knowledge regarding saving, building assets, investing, and leaving money to your children when you pass.

For example, most people I knew growing up had no idea of how to leave an inheritance using life insurance. People think that life insurance is only used to cover the cost of the funeral. They do not see it as a way to pass down wealth to their children as well. Even then, most people will still never end up getting life insurance but instead leave the bill for end of life costs to their family members.

In most cases, those family members will be left with no choice but to borrow money from elsewhere or start a GoFundMe fundraiser, asking help if they cannot afford to pay for the funeral costs. The problem here is a lack of education. If only they knew that by paying a monthly premium each month (lower than some of their bills), they could ensure that a significant amount of money will be given to their children when they pass away. The other thing to be understood about life insurance is that some factors must be met for the money to be given by the life insurance company.

For instance, your life insurance company might not payout your policy if you die of a specific illness, but it will payout if you die of some other kind of disease or accident that is not mentioned in their policy. You must read all the terms in your life insurance policy and understand everything (for example, see if they pay out if you decided to take your own life). Do not just sign anything before you compare prices, especially when you are signing your mortgage papers. They will offer you life insurance but shop around and see what else is out there. Once you've done this, compare and see if what the banks offer you makes sense for you and your family. It's critical that you make sure that you never miss a payment as well. It's better to use your last dollar and pay your monthly premium because by doing that, you know that you are helping in securing your children's future. They won't have to ever decide between either paying their insurance premium or the electrical bill because you will have sacrificed for them today to ensure that they have enough money to never worry about that.

Most people are never taught at a young age how to properly buy an investment property, stocks, or how to keep money circulating within their community. These are just a few of the things that are not taught in typical minority households. Generational wealth isn't only about passing down finances, assets, or businesses. It's also about passing down things like education, great genes, and good health practices. If a child grows in an environment where eating healthy is a priority, then chances are they will grow up doing the same and pass those habits down to their kids. These practices will help your children's overall health and, most likely, their children's health will be in good standings as well.

It's important to remember this one thing: how important can wealth be without good health? In this book I want to show you, and anyone reading this book, some of the things that children are not being taught in our current school system. These are basic things that all parents should be teaching their children because no one else will teach them. This information is vital to their financial success. Unfortunately, sometimes parents grew up in the same system that doesn't teach them these vital things. The fact that no one ever taught them any of these things makes passing down this knowledge extremely challenging but not impossible.

This factor is the other primary reason why I decided to write this book. I want to pass down all the information that I have learned to you and anyone reading this book in hopes that one day this book and the information within it will be passed down for many generations to come. In this book, I will be focusing on using real estate to help build your wealth and legacy, which you will pass down to your children's children.

CHAPTER 2

Why Real Estate Is a Great Tool for Building Generational Wealth

D ear children, as you get older, you will soon realize that there are many ways that you can make money with in this world. By the time you read this, the world might have drastically changed, and some of the things that I am about to tell you might not be relevant. The information I am about to give you, on the other hand, has been relevant for centuries and has made a lot of people millionaires.

The three main reasons why there aren't a lot more millionaires in this world today is due to the lack of education, opportunity, and income. These three factors have made it extremely hard for people to execute the steps needed to become wealthy. The good thing is that the world is changing and in a positive way. The average Joe can now become wealthy, even without much of an education or a large amount of income. This chapter will be discussing why real estate is an excellent investment and a great tool for building generational wealth.

When it comes to real estate, there are a lot of ways you can invest. For example, you can buy houses to fix up then sell them at a profit. Some people will buy the stocks of companies that buy, and own real estate called REITS (Real Estate Investment Trusts). Other people buy houses and rent them out. You can also get into purchasing commercial real estate and apartment buildings. The point is that there are many ways you can get into real estate investing.

In my opinion, I think the best approach is to buy rental properties. I truly believe that this is the best way to build and keep generational wealth. Keep in mind that this is the year 2020, and by the time you read this book, many things could have changed. For example, today, it was announced that anyone who doesn't produce a down payment of twenty percent or higher on an investment property would face tight restrictions. They also made it harder to qualify for a traditional mortgage by ensuring your credit score has to be at least 680. In the previous year, the minimum credit score you need to have to qualify for a loan was 600.

They are also adjusting the debt to income ratio qualifications (debt to income ratios will be explained in the next chapter). The worst adjustment they made, which will impact many investors, is that you can only refinance your multifamily property when you need to use the money to make improvements on that specific property. This new rule applies unless you make a down payment of over twenty percent. These adjustments came about due to the Coronavirus, which has put the whole world on lockdown.

Again, by the time you read this, many other things might have changed, but using real estate as your generational wealth builder will still remain valid. That is why it's essential to make sure you are always researching and networking. The economy is ever-changing, and new opportunities and tools are always popping up, so make sure you take advantage of them. Keep in mind that each country, state, and province have their own rules and regulations. That is why it's important to do your research.

The first reason I think buying a rental property is a great way to build generational wealth is simple. What other type of investment can you put down twenty percent or less of an asset's total value, then get someone else to pay off the balance? What I mean by this is, you are only putting down a small fraction of the total cost of something from your own pocket. You are then borrowing the rest to come up with to total amount you need to buy the asset.

The beauty part is that the renter will be the one paying back the total amount that you borrowed and not you. While the amount is getting paid down by the renter, you actually have ownership rights to that property. You can even get your initial investment out by refinancing the property and repeating the cycle. The fact that you can put down twenty percent or less and the renters end up paying off the remaining eighty percent over time is outright fantastic.

Another amazing thing is that you have ownership rights to the property during this whole time, which you can use as financial leverage elsewhere if you wish to. You can also get your initial investment out by adding value to the house. You can do this for example, by adding extra bedrooms or doing anything to the property that will increase its value on the market. This is called forced appreciation. When you combine forced appreciation with the fact that property values naturally go up over time, and you add how much money the renters have paid down on your loan so far, this will be the money you can get out in cash (referred to as equity) when you refinance your mortgage. When you refinance your mortgage, you are basically taking out a new loan to pay your old loan off and you pocket the difference. Refinancing can free up your initial investment, which you can now use to buy more property, start a business, invest, etc.

When purchasing rental properties, make sure that they also give you what is called a positive cash flow (I will talk more in-depth about this in a future chapter). You are getting someone else to pay down the loan for you each month with the rent they pay you. It's almost like they pay you each month for that opportunity to make you and your family wealthy. Renters trade their time for money at work each week so they can give you a portion, which in turn allows you to have more free time on your hands. This arrangement builds your empire and grows your wealth.

Renters become your employee, but you don't pay them. Instead, they pay you in cash each month for the opportunity to work for your empire. Ensure that you save that positive cash flow every month because it will help you maintain your property and help you buy more real estate. It's also essential to keep that cash flow because it will give you peace of mind. You will know that you are covered and will not have to spend out of your pocket to pay for unforeseen expenses if anything happens.

The second reason I think buying a rental property is a great way to build generational wealth is that property throughout human history tends to increase in value over time. The house you buy today will be worth more money in the future. It makes sense because the amount of habitable land in the area you want to buy in will always be limited. Therefore, as more houses get built, less land becomes available for future real estate development. This is true all over the world because the earth only has so much land on it. The supply eventually will hit its capacity and, in turn, drive up the demand. The longer you own the property, the more money it will be worth, which is good for accumulating generational wealth. The critical thing to remember is that, like stocks, the price of real estate fluctuates due to a lot of factors like supply and demand, the state of the economy, things being built close by, etc. Although the housing market does fluctuate, it does so in an upward trend over time. This type of increase over time is called appreciation.

The third reason I believe buying rental properties is a great way to build generational wealth is because of the tax benefits ownership gives you. The easiest way for me to explain how taxes work is to give you an example. If I were to make fifty thousand dollars in a year at a regular job and someone else were to make the same amount with their rental properties, guess who gets to pay fewer taxes on that fifty thousand dollars. The person who made fifty thousand dollars using their rental properties would get to keep more of their money. Due to the fact that their income was generated through rental income, the current laws state that you can deduct things like property depreciation, property taxes, mortgage interest, and other thing related to real estate. In turn, this will allow you to pay less in taxes and keep more of your money. I don't want to get into too many details about taxes and how they work with regards to rental properties because, by the time you read this, as I said before, they might have different tax laws than they do today. Make sure to talk to an accountant about this and also do your own research.

The fourth reason buying a rental property is a great way to build generational wealth is that if you purchase real estate at a price lower than what the market is currently asking for it, you will already have equity built into the property. Equity is how much the house can be sold in today's market versus how much you currently owe on that property. Equity factors in how much of the principal you paid down on your loan so far. For example, if you purchased a rental property for $100,000 and that same exact type of property sells for $110,000 in the same area, you can get your house appraised and possibly have $10,000 in equity.

This is all possible because a house just like yours, in the same area, sold for much more than what you paid for it. Then let's say your renters have been paying down your mortgage for the past five years, and now you owe $30,000 less on your mortgage. When you add the $10,000 and $30,000 together, it will give you $40,000 in total equity. The great thing about having equity in a property is you can use it as leverage to borrow money to help you get more properties, start a business, send your kids to school, etc. To recap everything so far, you will be receiving money from your renters, which reduces the amount you owe on the property each month. You also made sure that you bought the rental property at a discount. These two things help increase the equity in your property, not including the fact that your property will increase in value over time.

As I mentioned before, you can also increase the equity on your property by using forced appreciation. Forced appreciation is accomplished by renovating your property So when an appraiser (the person who determines the worth of your property) comes and sees all the improvements you have done, he or she will increase your property's value. The major thing to keep in mind about forced appreciation is that you have to make major changes. Adding an additional room, finishing the basement, adding a garage, or installing a deck is likely to get your property value to increase a significant amount. Another thing you also what to think about when doing these renovations is that when your property value goes up, so do your property taxes.

There are other reasons why rental properties are a great way to build generational wealth, but the four listed above are the main reasons. The other reasons include the fact that if something terrible happens to the house, you still own the land. It's an investment that you can see, feel, smell, and control. I am sure by now, some people reading this will argue that investing in stocks might be a better way of building generational wealth or maybe even starting a business. To them, I say, how many times have people lost all of their life savings in the stock market or investing in companies, compared to real estate.

Currently, a large number of businesses have shut down entirely during this coronavirus pandemic, and not just your regular mom and pop businesses; I am talking about large corporations. Oil future stocks went below zero, and a lot of people lost a ton of money there. The one thing that remains true is that all those employees, CEOs, and stockbrokers all need a place to live. That's why real estate has made a lot of people millions and billions of dollars throughout human history. Remember, even though real estate prices might fluctuate, it's always doing so in an upward direction over time.

CHAPTER 3

How to Qualify for a Home Loan

Dear children, now it's time to get into the practical side of everything. It's time to talk about the important steps that you need to take to start your real estate journey on the right path. The first step is to have the right mindset about real estate. I hope the two chapters before this one helped you to get there and see the bigger picture. One thing that I have learned thus far in life is that to be truly successful at anything, your "why" has to be your biggest motivator. Your "why" must be bigger than your self-gratification. When I talk about your "why," I am talking about the real reason you are doing what you are doing. Your "why" will help you during the toughest of times to continue to push forward and never give up no matter how bad the situation gets because your why is greater than your suffering.

The second step is to see where you stand when it comes to your credit score. I genuinely hope that by the time you read this, your credit score is at least an eight hundred because your mother and I would have taught you how to accomplish this before turning eighteen. If your credit score isn't eight hundred or more, don't worry, there are many things you can do to increase it. I remember a time when my score was in the low 500's. I was young and didn't understand how credit worked. My credit cards were almost always maxed, and I had to add money to my credit card just to use them. Even with all that, I increased my credit score over time, and your mother and I managed to purchase our first property. You will need to research how to increase your credit score, or if you don't have any credit, you will need to find out how to get credit.

There are many resources you can use to help you with your credit score. I could write another book on the different ways to do this, but they might be outdated by the time you're reading this. They also could be different depending on the country you are living in, but this is why I always insist on doing your research.

This book is like the road that will lead you to the bigger picture. Keep in mind that over time, new roads will form that will lead you to the same destination, or maybe this current road will need to be reconstructed over time. You might encounter some roadblocks along the way. That's why it's essential to keep up with changes and do your research no matter what.

With that said, here are a couple of things you can do to maintain a good credit score. Ensure that you pay your bills on time and don't use more than twenty percent of your credit limit. Also, keep your credit cards running for a long time to reflect a consistent payment history. Try to have different types of credit but remember not to apply for any other loans a couple of months before applying for your home loan. Applying for a loan beforehand will drastically drop your credit score and affect your home loan chances. If you already have the cash to purchase that rental property yourself, you won't have to worry about some of the things I discuss in this chapter.

On the other hand, remember that it is sometimes better to get a loan and save your own money. This way, you use other people's money (the bank, private investors, etc.) to build your empire. The bank is your business partner, especially when you get a loan from them. They are the ones putting in the majority of the money to fund your deal, which means that you will need to prove to the bank that you can make your payments on time. Your payment history will help them gauge the likelihood of you paying them back fully, including all the interest they will be charging you. Your credit score helps them figure out how reliable you are as a business partner. The higher your score, the more credible you are, making it easier for them to give you a loan.

Although the banks are your partners, remember that they are making a lot of money off you. They make sure that they are always protected, and very rarely do they lose all their money when dealing with home loans. By the time you finish paying for your property, the banks will have collected three times, if not more, the amount of the original loan from you. On an average thirty-year mortgage, you will be paying more of the interest than the principal (the amount that you originally borrowed from the bank to purchase the house). This will be the case until about year twenty of a thirty-year loan. You can use an amortization calculator to determine when more of your monthly mortgage payments will be going towards your actual loan (principal) than paying the interest. Mortgage calculators can be found all over the internet and in app stores. This is an example of when your 'why' comes into play. You understand that you will pay for your house probably three times over before your amortization period ends, but it is the cost you pay to build your empire. If your 'why' is big enough, you will need to have this type of mindset. The good thing is you will get other people (renters) to pay for the property anyway.

The third step is that you need to make sure that your debt-to-income ratio is low. To achieve this, you need to ensure that the amount you pay toward your debts each month is lower than the amount you make each month. You don't want to have a lower income than the amount you pay back towards your debt. To calculate your debt-to-income ratio, you need to add up all the payments you make monthly towards your debt. This includes anything that's on your credit report, including anything in collections (if any) and also include any child support payments if you have any. Then you add up all of your useable gross income. Gross income is the money you get before taxes are taken out. For your income to qualify as useable income, you will have to be working at the same job or in the same industry for at least two years. Remember that these standards might change over time or might differ depending on the country you live in, so it is essential to do your research and talk to your mortgage broker to make sure the income you want to use is deemed usable.

Once you have your total debt payments and your applicable gross income, you now have to account for the new mortgage payments you will start paying if you get approved for the loan. Your mortgage broker will help you determine your mortgage payments, which depends on the following: the interest rates that they are offering you, the cost of the property, if it is a fixed or variable rate, and your down payment amount. You then add your new mortgage payments to your total debt payments, divide that number by your useable gross income to get your debt-to-income ratio.

Let me give you an example of how this will work using some numbers. Let's say your monthly minimum credit card payment is $200.00, and your car payments and student loan payments are $800.00 per month. Your current monthly debt is $1,000.

You then go to your mortgage broker because you found a property that you want to buy. Let's say he or she tells you that your monthly mortgage payments will be $2,200 per month, including the monthly taxes and insurance. When you add this to your current monthly debt of $1,000, your total monthly debt will now be $3,200. In this example, we will say that your total usable monthly income is $8,000, which can include your partner's income and anyone else who will be on the mortgage. Remember that the equation for calculating your debt-to-income ratio is your total debt payments per month divided by your usable monthly income. Using this example to calculate your debt to income ratio, you divide $3,200 by $8,000. Your answer will be 0.4, and you will need to multiply this number by 100 to get a percent. Therefore, the total debt to income ratio for this example will be 40 percent.

Currently, a debt-to-income ratio under 35% is considered good. However, remember that by the time you read this, the standard could have changed. Anything above 35% could mean you might not qualify, depending on the type of loan you are applying for. Remember, you can play around with the total usable income by adding other people onto the loan if you have to or by using your business income as well. There are a couple of different ways you can decrease your debt to income percentage like paying off some old debt etc. Make sure to talk to your mortgage broker about this. It's in their best interest for you to qualify for the loan because if you do, that means they get paid as well.

The fourth step you need to take is to ensure that you have enough money to cover your closing costs and down payment. Additionally, you have to make sure that you have enough money left over to cover your regular lifestyle bills. Some lenders even look at how long your money has been sitting in your savings account. Closing costs differ from place to place, depending on where you are buying your property. Closing costs include land transfer tax, lawyer fees, property appraisal fees (if needed) and possibly inspection fees. The seller also has their expenses to pay, including paying for the real estate agent who showed you (the investor) the property. For now, we will just focus on you as the buyer. Closing costs, on average, are about five percent of the purchase price. Remember, this is different depending on where you are buying and the type of deal you are structuring. You will have to do research and talk to your real estate agent, lawyer, and mortgage broker to estimate the total closing costs in that area.

Once you have mastered the steps above, getting a loan shouldn't be a problem. A unique situation you might find yourself in will be if you end up buying multiple properties. In this situation, that means that your debt-to-income ratio will increase. The good thing is if you rent out those properties, then the money you get from the tenants can be considered as usable income as well, which allows you to buy more properties. Eventually, the banks will simply say no to you getting a new loan with them because you have too much money borrowed out, even if your debt to income ratio is still good. At this point, you will have to start looking at private lenders, hard money lenders, partners, or finding other creative ways to fund your deals (I will talk about these creative ways in a future chapter).

The only problem with private lenders or hard money lenders is that their interest rates are higher than what the banks would offer, which will negatively affect your profits. A creative way to fund your project would be to do what's called a syndication, which requires getting a group of people to invest with you. These investors will combine their money with yours, and in return, you will give them a portion of the profits each month or year. Most investors like to see a return on their investment of at least 15 percent. Syndications usually work well with multi-unit properties to come up with the down payment.

On the other hand, you can buy house out right with the type of money used to pay the down payment on a multi-unit apartment. By doing this, you avoid using any banks, but unfortunately, you won't be leveraging your money. I will talk more about other creative ways that you can fund your deal without using the banks and the power of leveraging your money in the upcoming chapters.

One question that you might have is that if you keep getting loans to buy these properties and pass away, are you not just leaving your debt to your children? One solution to solving that problem is to get a life insurance policy that will leave your children enough money to pay off the majority of the properties you own, if not all of them. You can even use the rental income you get from the properties you own to help pay your monthly payment on your insurance policy. Worst case scenario, if your insurance company doesn't want to pay your family after you pass for whatever reason, then you will still have that rental income coming in every month to help cover the expenses. Your loved ones can also use this money to help support their lifestyle while paying down the mortgages. They might only have to keep the property for an additional ten years or less before it's all paid off. There are other ways you can protect your family, but I just wanted to show you that this can be done as long as you do your research, take action and talk to an accountant.

CHAPTER 4

How to Select a Cash-Flowing Property

D ear children, at this point, I am sure you have gone to a mortgage broker and figured out how much you have been pre-approved for. The next step in this process is one of the most critical steps you have to understand regarding real estate investing. It helps to ensure that you select the right type of property to invest in, and allows you to identify the purchase price that makes sense to ensure your cash flow.

The average person who starts investing in real estate begins with single-family homes. They might even house hack (house hacking is a term used to identify a situation where a homeowner is staying in the same house they are renting). They can either rent room-by-room or rent out the basement while they live upstairs or the other way around. Single-family homes will help give you the first-hand landlord experience. It's a great way to get started because managing and maintaining a single-family home is easier than a multifamily property, especially if you stay in the same house.

If a problem comes up in a single-family home, it might cost you about $2,000 to fix, but the same problem in a 200-unit apartment building might cost you $400,000. The more experience you get with single-family real estate, the more knowledge and skills you will obtain to help you invest in multi-unit apartments, commercial and other types of real estate. Keep in mind that if you start by investing in a multi-unit apartment first, it's okay as long as you do your research, understand the risks, and have the right amount of cash in reserve.

In this chapter, I'll give you the calculations needed to help you analyze if the real estate property you want to buy will be a good investment for you or not. I will walk you through an example, and at the end of this chapter and show you all the calculations. You can use these calculations for any type of property you are trying to analyze.

Okay, so let's say, for this example, you found a two-story house with a legal basement suite, and it's in your price range. You now need to do the math to figure out if this house will be a good investment for you or not. The cost of the house is $365,000. The top unit is renting out for $1,900, and the basement unit is renting out for $1,800. Your total rental income will be $3,700. As a long-term real estate investor, you want to make sure that your properties cash-flows every month. Cash flow is the amount you have left over after you pay off all the expenses with the money you are getting from your tenants. It's the profit that you have at the end of each month after paying for things like mortgage, taxes, insurance, repairs, utilities, and property manager fees are paid.

An excellent way to figure out if a property has good potential cash flow is to use what's called the one percent rule. The one percent rule is a rule of thumb you can use to quickly determine if a particular property has a high probability of generating a positive cash flow. Use it only as a guide; just because it passes the one percent rule doesn't mean it will cash-flow. There are other factors you need to look at as well. If a property passes the one percent rule, that means there is a high probability that your property will cash-flow after all expenses are paid. For a property to pass the one percent rule, the total amount charged for rent has to be one percent of that property's purchase price.

Our example above shows that the full rental income is $3,700, and our purchase price is $365,000. To satisfy the one percent rule, we need to figure out what one percent of $365,000 is and then see if the rental income is above that number. To calculate that, you multiply $365,000 by 0.01, and you get $3,650. Since your rental income is $3,700 (which is above the $3,650), it does satisfy the one percent rule. Therefore, this property passed the first step in determining if a property is a good investment or not. If it didn't pass the one percent rule, I wouldn't dismiss it altogether. I would have to look into what caused it not to pass the one percent rule and see if there is a way around it.

Sometimes properties won't pass the one percent rule because the rents being charged are lower than the going market rate, which means you can increase the rents, and maybe then it will fit the one percent rule. Any property that doesn't satisfy the one percent rule will have a red flag in my head. Everything else has to be just right for me to consider it a potential investment. Remember that just because a property passes the one percent rule doesn't mean that it's a great investment. You will have to look at other factors as well to help you make that decision.

For example, if you purchase a property and then realize that you have to do some renovations before renting it out. Those renovation costs will need to be added to your purchase price, which could cause your property not to pass the one percent rule due to the extra money you have to put in before renting it out. Keep in mind that the one percent rule is only there to help you quickly assess if a property has the potential to cash-flow. It doesn't always guarantee that the property will cash-flow. Some investors actually use a two percent rule or higher to give themselves a little more of a cushion just in case they miss something.

If the property passes the one percent rule, you now have to take a deeper look into all the expenses associated with this property to determine if it still produces a positive cash flow. You will have to do your research and find documentation showing the actual expenses each month. Do not just go by what the seller is telling you.

In the example we are using, we will look at a couple of different expenses that need to be accounted for to see if the property truly cash-flows each month. These expenses are your mortgage payments, taxes, insurance, and the amount to be saved each month to account for any vacancies. It also includes the amount to be saved each month for possible repairs and maintenance, utilities, snow removal, lawn care, homeowner association fees (if needed), capital expenditure, and property manager fees. When it comes to figuring out how much to save each month to cover vacancies, I like to say save anywhere from ten to twenty percent of the rental income for this, but you need to already have some cash in reserves from the first day you purchase the property. For general repairs and maintenance, I recommend saving five percent of your rental income.

Capital expenditure is the amount you need to save for big renovations, maintenance, and purchases like the AC unit, washer, dryer, fridge, furnace, dishwasher, and roof. They don't need to be replaced often, but when you need to replace them, they cost a lot of money. Your home insurance can cover some of these things (depending on the insurance you get) but you will still need to pay your deductible. I recommend saving at least five percent of your rental income for this. Your property manager will generally charge anywhere between eight to twelve percent of your rental income each month. To find out how much taxes you will have to pay each month, call the city hall. They will have that information for you.

Your mortgage broker will be able to give you more information on how much your mortgage payments will be each month. To find out how much home insurance you will be spending each month, I recommend talking to an insurance broker. They can give you different quotes from multiple insurance companies and help you select the right insurance. Hopefully, you will be passing on the utilities to your tenants, but you will still need to know how much they cost. You can also add the utility cost into the rent and advertise the property as utilities included, which will help you rent out the place faster. You can call the local gas, electric, and water companies in the area to get a quote on the average cost of the utility bills, or you can get a copy of the tenant's bills for the past couple of months if they allow you.

When it comes to lawn care and snow removal, you can look up companies online to get the cheapest quote. You will only need to do this if you do not pay for homeowner association (HOA) fees. I strongly recommend not buying a house that has an HOA. Their fees can randomly go up at any point, which can mess with your monthly profits. On the other hand, there are a lot of people out there that invest in properties with HOA fees and are successful. It's just not something I am comfortable taking a risk on, but do your research on that specific HOA and make an informed decision. Keep in mind that each country, state, and province might have its own rules and regulations on HOA fees, which is why it's important to do your research.

Now that you have calculated your monthly expenses, you will need to calculate your net operating income (NOI) that you will be getting each month. Net operating income doesn't include your mortgage payment or income taxes. It's the money you make after all expenses are paid, excluding your mortgage and before your income tax. To calculate this, you subtract all your expenses besides your mortgage and the taxes you will pay from your rental income. Your mortgage and taxes are not included in this calculation because it will help you compare one property to another on the same playing field.

The amount you pay in taxes depends on many factors including your location. Everyone has different tax payment structures, and your mortgage payments will depend on your interest rate, the amount you put down, and other factors. All this makes it hard to compare one place to another, but it helps give you a better picture when you remove these variables. I like to add the mortgage payment and taxes so that I can get a real picture of what my monthly cash flow will be. If your number is positive for the property you are analyzing, this means that this property has positive cash flow and can be considered a potentially good investment.

However, other things need to be looked at before a property can be deemed a good investment. Some of these things include the property's location, the average appreciation of properties in the area over a few years, growth within the area in the past years, and future growth projections.

The next thing you will need to calculate is your yearly profit, which will help you see how much cash flow you will have each year. To calculate this, you multiply your cash flow each month by twelve because there are twelve months in a year. The other calculation you need to do is your cash-on-cash return on investment. A cash-on-cash calculation helps you understand how much money your initial investment is generating for you each year. For example, if you put $20,000 in a savings account, how much will it grow each year? The answer is it will depend on the interest rate that that savings account is offering you.

When it comes to real estate and other investments, to figure out how much your initial investment will grow each year, you have to determine what your cash-on-cash return will be. To calculate your cash-on-cash return, you take your yearly profit and divide it by your initial investment. Then multiply it by 100 to get a percent. Your initial investment should include every bit of money you put in to purchase the property. Including your down payment, closing cost, inspector fees, and anything you needed to fix before it meets your move-in standard. The last calculation you will need that I believe is important will determine your cap rate.

Cap rates are used to help you compare properties all over the world, and it's used mostly with large multifamily properties. It's used to help determine the potential return and risk that one property can give you compared to another. Keep in mind that cap rates don't include expenses like taxes, mortgages, depreciation, whether or not the building is fully occupied. Cap rates also do not include if the current rents are up to the current market rents, market rent potential growth, capital expenditures, location of the property, and the final sale price if you decide to sell the property. You can buy a property with a higher cap rate compared to another, but maybe, over time, the property with a lower cap rate area improves. When you decide to sell the property, the one with the initial lower cap rate might sell at a higher price than the one with a higher one. In this case, you were better off investing in a property with a lower cap rate than a higher one because your return on investment is now better with the property with the initial lower cap rate.

To calculate a cap rate, you take your net operating income and divide it by the price you paid to purchase the property, then multiply that number by 100 to get a percentage. You can now compare the cap rate of one building to another and quickly identify which property between the two (or however many you are analyzing) is most likely to give you the best return on your investment.

Once you have all the information about what a cap rate doesn't include, you will need to use an internal rate of return (IRR) to get a more accurate return rate on your investment. The internal rate of return also lets you know how quickly your invested money is coming back to you. The faster you get your money back, the faster you can use that money to help fund another deal.

In order to determine if a property is worth investing in or not, it is important that you use all these calculations together to get a true understanding of your return on investment. Do not use just one of these calculations alone and think you have done your due diligence. It's important to step back and view all the numbers you get from these calculations, then make a sound, calculated, and informed decision based on these numbers as well as other factors.

Another thing that you need to do which doesn't involve calculations, but will help you select a cash-flowing property, is to understand the market the property rents in. You need to know where the market rents are today and what they are projected to be in the future. You will also need to know how much rent the current tenants are paying. With this information, you can then decide if you want to do renovations or not. It's important to keep in mind that if you go above and beyond and add top-of-the-line fixtures in an area that doesn't support the high-end rents, you would have wasted your money. It's equivalent to you walking into a house located in a great area with gold bathrooms and expensive kitchen appliances, which rents out at a high price. Then thinking that if you install the same gold bathrooms and expensive kitchen appliances in a property located in an area were the market rents are lower, you should be able to get the same high-end rents there as well. It just doesn't work that way. That's why it's important to know your market and understand how much people in that area are paying for their rents. Additionally, you should know what the average salary is in that area is.

You will also have to do research and see what the expected growth in that market is projected to be, as it will help you determine what the future potential rents will be. If you decided to do renovations, make sure that you hire the right people to give you an accurate cost analysis on the project because renovations cost a lot. You need to get an accurate quote in order to determine if the property is worth buying or not. Underestimating this will cause you to lose money and possibly acquire a property that doesn't cash-flow. The calculations that I listed above, to me, are the most important calculations that you need to know to help you determine if a property is a possible great investment or not. You can use other calculations like determining the effective gross income, but if you understand the calculations above first, you are heading in the right direction. Remember to talk to an accountant and always do your research.

Below I have outlined these calculations step-by-step, using an example of a property that costs $365,000. It's important to note that I am not an accountant and that you must consult with a qualified accountant to help you through this type of analysis.

Consulting an accountant will ensure that your numbers are correct, and you have included all your variables.

Cost for House:	$365,000

Rent per Unit

Unit 1	Top Unit	$1900.00
Unit 2 Basement Unit		$1800.00
Total		$3,700.00

One Percent Rule: Rent must be a minimum of 1% of the cost of the house
365,000 x 0.01 = $3,650 (This property passed the 1% rule)

Expenses per Month

Mortgage:	$1805.00
Taxes:	$200.00
Insurance:	$94.00
Vacancy: (10% of rental income)	$370.00
Repairs/maintenance: (5% of rental income)	$185.00
Utilities: (water, sewer, gas, electricity, garbage)	$250.00
Lawn/snow care	$40.00
HOA Fees	$0.00
Capital Expenditure (Saving for major repairs @ 5%)	$185.00
Property Manager: (10%)	$370.00
Total (Assuming renters pay for all utilities)	Total: $3,499.00

- **Net Profit** per Month = Income (Rent + other income) – Total Monthly Expenses
  Net Profit =$3,700 - $3,499 = $ 201
  Yearly Profit = Net profit x 12
  Yearly Profit = 201 x 12= $2,412
- **Cash on Cash** return on investment = Net Profit per month (after all expenses paid) x 12 divided by own money you put in (down payment, closing cost, inspector, capital expenditure, mortgage, taxes, etc.) x 100.
  Cash on Cash return = Annual cash flow/ Total Investment X 100
  Cash on Cash return on investment = 2.412 X 100 = 10.72%
  (5% down payment plus closing costs at $4,000) $22,500
- **Net operating Income** = Total rental income minus all expenses not including mortgage, capital expenditure and taxes = $3,700 – $1,309 = $2,391
- **Cap Rate percent** = yearly profit (net operating income)/cost for house x 100
  $2,391/$365,000 X 100= 0.65 % (Generally good Cap rates are between 6% and up)

CHAPTER 5

Understanding the Risks Around Real Estate Investing

Dear children, whenever you invest in anything, understand that it always comes with some form of risk. Investing in real estate isn't an exception. Every time you borrow money to buy a property, there is always the risk that you might not be able to make your mortgage payments for whatever reason, and your property could be taken away. For example, what happens when your renters don't pay their rent, and they still decide to stay there until you evict them? It can lead to you losing months' worth of rental income. What happens when Mother Nature decides to destroy your house, and your insurance company refuses to pay for the damages? These are just a few things to consider when purchasing a property.

On the other hand, the rewards are so much greater. Building generational wealth propels you and your family financially in this world. That's why real estate investors are willing to take the risk. In this chapter, I will be talking about the different types of risks associated with real estate investing.

One of the risks that you have to be aware of when investing in real estate is that real estate lacks diversification. What I mean by this is, let's say you wanted to buy stocks, you have the option of buying only technology type of stocks, energy stocks, or you can combine both. Stocks are diversified. You are still buying stocks, but the stocks themselves can be diversified so that if something happens with the energy market and your energy stocks drop, at least you won't lose all your money because your technology stocks will still be doing good.

When it comes to real estate, if something happens in the housing market and it crashes (like the 2008 housing crash), it won't matter what type of real estate you own. You are going to get affected somehow if your properties are in that area. Most likely, your property value will drop, but you might be able to raise your rents over time due to more people needing to rent where they live instead of buying. Many people lost their real estate empires in the housing crash of 2008, and it didn't matter if they had single-family homes or multi-unit apartments. Everyone was affected because investing in real estate lacks diversification. It's also hard to get your money out when dealing with real estate compared to other types of investments like stocks. Purchasing real estate means you will lack liquidity, which can be a problem when faced with a crisis. There is a way to get around the liquidity problem (by investing in REITs), but I will discuss that in a different chapter.

Another risk you have to be aware of when dealing with real estate investing is when you do not give yourself enough of a safety margin. When purchasing any property, it is critical that you buy it much lower than the market value. It gives you a margin of safety because even though you run your numbers and everything on paper looks good, things like the housing crash of 2008 can happen any time. When things like this do happen, and you have managed to give yourself a reasonable margin of safety, it will increase your probability of weathering the storm and keeping your asset.

We are humans and prone to making mistakes, but having a margin of safety allows us to buffer some of these mistakes. People will sometimes attempt to "make the numbers work" when they are analyzing a deal. It might be because they are emotionally attached to the property. They want to make the deal work so badly that they are willing to give themselves a lower margin of safety to purchase it. Being emotional with any investment can be detrimental to your success. It's important always to stay true in processing and removing all emotions. Make all your decisions based on the numbers, all the factors surrounding the numbers, and never make decisions based on emotions. I know this can be difficult to do. Having someone or a team you can trust to run the numbers with you can help you in the long run.

Another risk that real estate investors have to deal with is what happens when you hire the wrong property manager, contractors, real estate agent, and accountant to be part of their team. If you are the investor and make the mistake of hiring the wrong person for any of these jobs, you will most likely lose a lot of money and possibly your asset. You must do extensive research and a detailed background check before hiring anyone for these jobs. Remember that you are the one responsible for everything that happens with each property that you own at the end of the day. Therefore, before you hire someone to do any job, you must already know how to do the job yourself or at least have a good idea. Having first-hand knowledge makes it easier for you to spot if something is wrong. Then when you confront whomever you hired about something, it's harder for them to mislead you.

Your property manager is one of the most important people you will hire because they will act on your behalf when you are not there. Your property manager is probably the person who can cause you to lose the most amount of money if you select the wrong person. I will list a couple of questions that you should ask a property manager before hiring them. It's critical that you interview as many property managers as you can and contact their references. You have to do this for anyone you want to hire for any of the positions I listed above.

The list of questions you should always ask your potential property manager goes as follows:

- Are you licensed?

- How do you screen potential tenants?

- What percentage of the monthly rent do you get?

- How do you handle evictions?

- How much do you charge to find renters?

- Who gets late fee payments when tenants are late with their rent?

- What services does your management contract include?

- And finally, if I am not happy with you, how much time is required to terminate the contract.

Another risk that real estate investors have to deal with is the possibility of getting sued. If someone slips and falls on one of your properties and gets hurt or, worse dies, then there is a high possibility that you will get sued. The best way to manage this risk is to make sure that you are doing everything in your power to avoid anyone from getting hurt on your property. Ensuring your pavements, walkways, and sidewalks are always clean, clear and shoveled is critical. Make sure to test the fire, smoke, and CO monitors in your properties regularly (documenting everything). Additionally, ensure all fire escapes, extinguishers, and elevators are serviced regularly. Take care of all complaints immediately and document everything.

Doing these things, and more, can and will help lower the chances of you getting sued. Another thing you can do is try and put your properties under a company (LLC). Make sure you talk to your bank before you do this because if you don't and you transfer the house deed to your LLC, it might trigger a due on sale clause (meaning you will have to pay the bank the remaining balance on the loan right away). Putting your properties in an LLC helps to protect your other personal assets from a lawsuit. You will also have to make sure that you have great insurance covering you for many different things because you never know what can happen on your property.

Real estate investors can also face the possibility that insurance or taxes will increase. For example, if your insurance or taxes go up, but your rental market remains the same, this could be detrimental to your investment calculations. A property that passed the one percent rule and was cash-flowing when you first got it might not be anymore because your expenses (in the form of taxes) went up. That's why it's essential to give yourself a reasonable margin of safety when doing your calculations.

One of the biggest risks that real estate inventors face is becoming over-leveraged. Over-leveraged means that you have borrowed money that you cannot even make the minimum monthly payments on. You have to make sure that you can make your monthly mortgage payments, even if, for some reason, all your tenants don't pay their rent for the next six to twelve months. The chances of that happening are low, but as we found out this year (2020), with the coronavirus putting the whole world at a standstill, anything is possible. This is why it's important to have cash reserves.

Real estate investors can quickly fall into this situation because each time they purchase a property, thousands (sometimes millions) of dollars were used to buy the asset. Unless they are purchasing the property in cash, they will have to borrow the money from another source. Since the property cost a lot of money to purchase, the amount they pay back monthly (interest and principal) will also be a relatively large amount. Due to the large mortgage payments investors have to make relative to their income or their cash reserves, they can easily become over-leveraged.

Using leverage is a great strategy when used the right way. The possibility of over-leveraging is why banks need to see your income statements and know about all your debt when you are applying for a loan. I will illustrate how leverage works using two different scenarios.

In the first scenario, let's say you have $100,000 in your bank account, and there is a property that is being sold for $100,000. If you don't use leverage, you will use the full $100,000 in your account to pay for the property, and you would own it outright.

In the second scenario, you will use leverage by only using $20,000 of the $100,000 in your account. You give a twenty percent down payment and borrow the rest from the bank, leaving you with 80,000 in your account. In both cases, you will own the deed to the property.

Now let's say you found three more properties worth $100,000, and you did the same thing you did in the second scenario by putting down $20,000 as a down payment. You will have a total of four properties and $20,000 still left in the bank. Over time let's say those properties appreciate by $10,000. In the first scenario, you would have made $10,000, but on the other hand, in the second scenario, you would have made $40,000. That is the power of leverage. The problem with leverage is that it can also go in the opposite direction. If property values drop by $10,000 and you used leverage to purchase your properties, you would be down $40,000 compared to $10,000 if you didn't use leverage in the example above. Keep in mind that real estate does fluctuate but in upward trend over time. This means eventually, your property value will increase, given the right amount of time.

There are other risks associated with real estate, and it all depends on the type of deal you are making to purchase the property and what your goal is for that property. The good thing with real estate is that the rewards are usually higher than the risks. Make sure to do your homework on each property and evaluate the risks involved before making the decision to purchase.

CHAPTER 6

Creative Ways to Fund Your Real Estate Purchases

D ear children, in order to build your real estate empire, you will need to purchase some form of real estate or at least invest in companies that focus on purchasing real estate. When dealing with physical real estate, you will be required to have the funds that the seller is requesting for the property. Once the seller's lawyer receives the funds, they will then transfer the deed over to you, which will give you the rights and ownership of that property. There can sometimes be a lengthy exchange between currency and real estate. Finding the right property usually is the easier part. The harder part is getting the capital to purchase the property (this has been my own experience. It might be the opposite for you).

Raising capital can be done in several ways. The most common way of achieving this is by saving up a down payment (the investor minimum is 20% of the purchase price) then borrowing the rest from the bank. Banks can lend you up to 80%

41

or more of the value of the property. You will have to come up with the remaining 20% or less for the down payment. Once you close the deal, you will be required to make monthly payments toward the amount you borrowed (the principal) plus the interest the bank is charging you. This method is the traditional way that most people pay for their properties.

In order to come up with the down payment for large real estate deals, some people use a home equity line of credit. If that is not enough, they can borrow the rest from an outside source, such as family members who give them money as a gift to help with the down payment. In this chapter, I will talk about different ways to fund your real estate deal to build your empire.

If you want to get into real estate and think that you are required to have thousands of dollars in your bank account, I am here to tell you that you can start investing in real estate with as little as one hundred dollars. In order to do this, all you will have to do is open a self-directed investing account. You can open one with your bank or use the cheaper platforms online that do not charge as much as the banks for buying and selling stocks. Once your account is active and funded, you can then use that hundred dollars to invest in Real Estate Investment Trusts (REITs) companies. They are traded just like stocks, making it easy for you to get your money in and out of your investment, unlike if you were to buy the property yourself.

This method is one of the ways you can invest in real estate and still be able to be liquid. The benefit of investing in a REIT is that you get all the benefits of owning real estate without managing tenants or the property, signing mortgage papers, paying for closing costs, and coming up with a down payment. The professionals who are hired by the REIT will take care of property management on your behalf. Simply put, each time the tenants pay their rents, you get a portion of that money, the amount depending on how much you invested. REITs are like stocks, but they must pay out the majority of their profits to the people who invest in them, unlike most stocks.

REITs pay their investors in dividends (distributions, if you are in Canada), but their tax structures are set up differently than most companies on the stock market. This structure is due to the fact that REITs don't pay corporate taxes. The profits they produce go straight to the investors and because of this, the REITs dividends are taxed higher than other stocks that give out dividends. That's important to know when you need to calculate your return on your investment when investing in a REIT. You will need to talk to a qualified accountant to help walk you through the steps because it depends on where you live. You need this information when filing your taxes. The best thing to do is to hold your REIT investment in a tax-free savings account to limit the amount of taxes you will have to pay.

Additionally, keep in mind that there are different types of REITs out there. For example, some REITs focus on commercial builds like malls, hospitals, nursing homes, and office buildings. Others will focus on providing mortgages, residential homes, land, and other types of real estate. REITs provide diversification within real estate because the REIT that you are investing in owns different types of property all over the world. So just like that, with as little as one hundred dollars, you can get started investing in real estate.

If stocks are not your cup of tea and you have enough capital, then one way you can fund your deal is to use your own money to pay for the full purchase of the property. Unfortunately, if you do this, you won't be able to leverage your money, as I discussed in the previous chapter. On the other hand, one good thing about paying for a property with your own money is that your monthly cash flow will be higher than to if you took out a loan on that property. You would have eliminated your biggest expense, which is your mortgage payments. When you buy a property with cash, you are guaranteed to get a lower purchase price than if you were to use financing to purchase the property. These two factors are why your monthly cash flow would be higher. This scenario means more money in your pocket per month than if you were to borrow money from somewhere else.

The reality is that most people cannot afford to buy real estate outright because they just don't have that excess amount of money laying around, and even if they did, most investors would prefer using leverage. That's why most investors have to borrow money from outside sources in order to purchase a property. These outside sources include banks, private lenders, and hard money lenders. Keep in mind that the banks offer a lower interest rate than the other sources, so those loans are more desirable and harder to get. Banks can offer you up to ten to fifteen percent lower interest rate than the other lenders, depending on how the economy is doing.

Hard money and private lenders will offer a higher interest rate because they know that in most cases, if you are going to them, then borrowing from the bank wasn't an option for you. They will also give you a shorter time frame to pay back the loan than the traditional banks. Although their interest is higher, they do, on the other hand, offer you the opportunity to purchase your property. It's better to have one percent of something than zero percent of nothing.

Another way you can fund your real estate deal is through a process called syndication. This allows you to take advantage of other people's money, credit, or experience to purchase a property. For example, let's say you find a great deal on investment property, and you don't have enough money to fund the purchase, but you know people that do. All you have to do is show them that the deal is solid with all the exact numbers, then, more than likely, they will agree to give you a portion of the money needed to purchase the property. In reality, this can be a lengthy and stressful process, especially if you don't have any experience.

However, once you convince enough people to combine their money with yours, then you should have more than enough funds to purchase the property. You will need to have a company set up that will hold the deed to the property and as well as the raised capital. The good thing about syndicating is that you can use the amount you raised towards only the down payment, or if you raise enough funds, you can use it to pay for the property outright (but remember the power of leveraging). If you are using it for a down payment, you can also leverage someone in the syndication group with a good credit rating to help secure the loan.

You can also add someone to the syndication just because they have experience maintaining the type of property you want to purchase. The ideal syndication team has people that are experienced in different fields related to real estate. This way, everyone in the team is adding value other than money, and they will manage whatever they are an expert in. You can also start a syndication where everyone is just bringing in the money, and you will be doing the rest. Remember to do your research on the legal way to structure a syndication. Keep in mind that each country, state, and province have their own rules and regulations, which is why it's important to do your research. Make sure to hire a lawyer who is experienced in the syndication process to guide you through everything. That is if you don't already have one who is part of your syndication team.

You can also fund your real estate deal through what's called owner financing (also known as seller financing). The only way that this works is if the person selling the house owns the house free and clear. The investor has either paid cash for the property or finished paying off the mortgage. At this point, the seller can now become the bank if they choose. The seller will transfer the deed to the buyer, and they will have full rights to the property. Its beneficial for the seller to use the owner financing system because they can negotiate for a higher selling price as well as charge a higher interest than a bank would. The seller also has the option to make the repayment period shorter than traditional banks if they wish. If you are unable to pay the seller at any time, then just like the bank, they get to keep the property and all the money you put in thus far. Seller financing benefits the buyer because, in most cases, your down payment to purchase the property will be lower than traditional banks, and sometimes you might not have to have one.

On the other hand, the interest rate and cost of the property will be higher. Most people who use this strategy to purchase a property have gotten rejected by traditional banks. This rejection could be due to a number of reasons like bad credit, high debt to income ratio, or other reasons. These investors normally don't want to use hard money lenders or other lenders due to their terms, so one of the only ways for them to get into the real estate game is to find deals with owner financing.

You will have to be careful when using this method because some sellers will charge extremely high interest rates and down payments in hopes that you will default on their loan contract. If you default on the loan contract, then the seller gets the house back and any money put into it so far. That's why it's important to note that if you are going to use this process, make sure you are doing your due diligence. Refer back to the chapter where I am talking about selecting a cash-flowing property and running your numbers to ensure you're getting a good deal. You might have to pay a higher purchase price and a higher interest rate, but you will get the opportunity to start building your empire. Make sure to talk to your financial advisor about this.

Another term to know when dealing with seller financing is called vendor take-back (VTB). Basically, the seller will give you a portion of the down payment required by the bank to qualify for a loan from the bank. In return, the seller will get monthly payments from you, which includes the interest and principal on the down payment loan they just gave you. It will be up to the seller to determine what interest they want to charge, and as long as you are cash-flowing at the end, it might be an option for you. The owner will also be put on the deed so that you cannot just sell the house without giving them back the money you borrowed from them. Once the amount they loaned to you is given back to them, they will be taken off the deed.

This scenario means you will have a second mortgage on the property. Therefore, you will be paying back the bank (or whatever lender) and the seller on a monthly basis. The problem you might face with this strategy is that some banks don't allow you to have a second mortgage on a property that they are funding. If that's the case, your best bet is to talk to your mortgage broker and let him or her find a bank that will allow for this type of transaction. It's important to note that there are different ways of incorporating the seller's capital into the deal. The main thing is that both the seller and you have to be comfortable with the deal's terms.

Another way to fund your real estate purchase is by using a lease to own option. It is similar to the owner financing option but with a few differences. With the lease to own option, you don't get to buy the property until the end of the lease, but with owner financing, you actually own the property on the first day. The lease to own option is mostly used for people who want to buy single-family homes, and the owner may not own the property outright.

It's structured to help people who don't have enough money for a down payment, have been rejected by banks, and don't have access to other private or hard money lenders. This option allows the investor to get into a property and rent it out for the lease duration. At the end (sometimes even during), the investor will have the option to buy the property, and the investor has time to do whatever they need to do to qualify for a loan during the duration of the lease. At the end of the lease, they have the option to buy the property, granted they qualify for a loan.

Lease-to-own options are structured differently, depending on the seller. It's beneficial to the investor because at least some of the money they are paying can go towards purchasing the property instead of renting somewhere else and trying to save at the same time. In this scenario, you can have part of the rent you pay per month to save for a down payment. The final selling price will be built into the agreement, making it a good option for anyone having a difficult time getting into real estate but needing to get in soon because they think the housing market will be increasing drastically. Additionally, it's a great option for the seller because they also don't have to worry about any maintenance costs or property manager costs, as the investor will be responsible for those.

The seller also benefits because now that property can have a higher cash flow per month, and the seller can structure the lease to last for however many years they want. Most of the time, leases last for about three to seven years, but again that's all up to the seller. The seller also doesn't have to pay for realtor fees if the investor decides to buy the property because they already have a buyer. In this case, the seller can save thousands of dollars in closing costs.

If, for some reason, the investor still cannot qualify for a loan after the lease is up, or they cannot find another way to pay the seller at the agreed-upon price, then the seller gets to keep all the money the investor has put into the deal so far. At this point, they can even kick the investor out of the property or start another lease option with them if they like. The seller's mortgage is also getting paid down during the leasing time frame as well, and more equity is getting built into that property for them by the investor (currently the renter).

It's important to note that you have to be really careful when choosing this option. Just like in the owner financing option, some sellers set up the lease option agreement with you in hopes that you default. Defaulting allows them to keep all the money and equity you built in the house. Most of the time (but not always), the lease option is set up in a way that you have to pay a non-refundable down payment or a portion of the down payment at the start. This amount is intended to go towards your down payment that you will need to qualify for a mortgage from a traditional bank. If you default on the agreement, then the seller will get to keep that money. So not only would you have paid rent that is way above the market rents and taken care of all maintenance, but you would also give up the thousands of dollars you put up as your non-refundable down payment. That's why it is critical that you make sure that you do everything in your power to qualify for a loan at the end of the lease option agreement. Use this option when you know you only have to do a few minor things in order to qualify for a bank loan. An option that you, as the investor, have is to get your lease option in place with the seller, then create another lease option with someone else and charge them a higher monthly rent than the original seller. You can then use the excess cash flow from this deal to help you save for your own down payment.

Another way to fund your real estate purchase is by using what's called a subject to contract. This contract allows you to take over the remaining payments on an existing mortgage. Let's say the original owner of the property can no longer make their mortgage payments for whatever reason, and their house is about to get foreclosed on. You, as the investor, can come in and take over their payments. You would be paying the current owner's mortgage payments on their behalf to the bank directly until the property is paid for in full. The contract will state that the owner will remain the mortgage owner, but the deed will be transferred over to you as the investor. This agreement allows you to rent the property or sell it, as long as the bank gets the amount owed to it by the closing date. Keep in mind that this is a contract between you and the current owner of the property, and the bank might not have any knowledge of the contract.

One of the risks involved with this option is that if you transfer the deed, the bank could request that the total amount left on the mortgage be paid to the bank right away, or they will be repossessing the property (this is referred to as the due-on-sale clause). The bank won't know that you have made this deal with the current owner, so as long as the payments continue to come in on time, the bank will be happy. It's critical that you talk to experts in this field before deciding to go for this option. If you wanted to, you could get the deed's transfer to happen when the mortgage is fully paid for, but the risk is the deed may remain in seller's name and not yours. This scenario could lead to lawsuits and other issues down the line, which is why, in most cases, the deed is transferred right away.

If you cannot make the payments to the house for some reason, the bank will hold the original owner of the property responsible, and that's a risk that the current property owner has to be okay with. Keep in mind that every five years or so, the term of the mortgage ends, and new rates will need to be renegotiated. Renegotiating requires the original owner of the mortgage to communicate with the bank every five years or so, depending on the mortgage terms you have with the bank. This issue is why this option doesn't work well for Canadian investors but works well for people in America because they have a fixed rate for their mortgage duration. If the seller decides to use this option, they have to understand that it will leave the seller with nothing, meaning all the money they put in the house is gone. This risk is why it's good to give the seller a good amount of cash up front.

However, the best thing is, as an investor, you will now have access to the equity that is in the house already. All the principal that was paid down on the mortgage will be yours (minus the cash that you paid upfront to the owner). Thus, if you structured the deal correctly, it will be like buying that house at a discount, and the current owner will also be glad to get the property that they couldn't afford off of their hands. The key thing you need to understand when using this method is to make sure that you know all the terms of the current owner's mortgage. Check to see how many payments they might be behind on, including taxes. You will also need to get the owner to add you to the house insurance as well. Make sure that you get an attorney that has specialized in subject to contracts.

Also, get the current owner to agree that you can claim the interest on the payments that you are making on your taxes and not theirs. One good thing about real estate is that you can deduct the interest payments you make to the bank on your taxes. Since you will be making the payment (the person or persons you rent the house to will be making the payments on your behalf), it only makes sense for you to claim them on your taxes. Make sure you consult with a tax specialist about this.

Ideally, you want to use this subject-to method if the majority of the mortgage has been paid for already. Remember, the bank could ask for the full repayment of the loan at any time if you transfer the deed. If you decide not to transfer the deed right away and wait until everything is paid for, you become vulnerable to lawsuits because, technically, you don't own the property. You will have to weigh the risks versus the rewards and determine if this is an option for you. People have used this method and made a lot of money, but at the same time, people have lost money as well. Make sure to do your research.

In conclusion, there are many other creative ways that you can use to fund your deals, but the key thing is always to understand the rules (laws). You also have to be okay with the terms and make sure that you are still cash-flowing at the end of the deal. When it comes to creatively funding your projects, the possibilities are endless. You could even partner up with someone who owns a property and use their house as collateral to help secure a loan from a bank for a bigger project. Don't let the lack of money stop you from making money.

CHAPTER 7

_____

Other Things You Need to Find Out Before Buying a Property

D ear children, there are a couple of key things that you need to know about any property before you purchase it. Knowledge of these things will help you determine if the property you are looking at is worth your investment. These key elements include, but are not limited to:

- Knowing the kind of traffic that is around the property.

- Knowing how old the property is.

- Knowing the average income in the area.

- Knowing cost of comparable properties in the same area.

- Knowing the type of zoning the property is in.

- Knowing what type of things are around or close to the property.

- Knowing the access to public transit.

These things are critical because they attract the types of renters you will want to live in your properties. In this chapter, I will discuss the things you need to know before you purchase a property.

It is important that you take the time to visit the property at different times and dates to get a good idea of what kind of traffic (foot and vehicle) is around the area. Some renters do not like areas where there is a lot of foot or vehicle traffic. Typically, the people who are okay with living in a noisy area where there is a lot of traffic are young professionals who don't have children. If young professionals are your target renters, then owning a property on a busy street won't be a problem for you. That's why it's important to visit the property as much as possible. Young professionals don't mind a little traffic and don't complain about the noise that much compared to other types of renters. They are driven to succeed and excel in their careers, which is great for the investor because it increases the possibility that they will pay their rents on time. Knowing the average income of the people in the area where your property is located is the second key thing you need to know before purchasing a property. It gives you an idea of the type of renters you will most likely be dealing with.

The third key thing you will need to know about a property before purchasing it is the property's age. This factor is important because knowing this allows you to predict what type of maintenance you might have to do before or after purchasing the property. For example, you know the average roof gets replaced every twenty to twenty-five years. If the property is twenty years old, and the roof hasn't been replaced before, then during the negotiation phase, you can use this as leverage to lower the purchase price.

It would be in your best interest to look at the furnace, the air conditioning units, electrical, plumbing, and any structural defaults that the house might have as well. Whoever inspects the property will give you information on most, if not all of these things. It's a good idea to have multiple inspections done with different inspectors specializing in the type of property you want to purchase. This step will help you get a better understanding of everything good and bad about the property.

Another key thing you will need to know about a property before you purchase it is the cost of comparable properties in the same area. You want to try to find a property that closely resembles yours. A comparable property will be in the same area as yours and have sold within a year or less. This information will help you gauge the current market value of the property. You can then use this information to help negotiate the price down if the property you want to buy is listed higher. This knowledge will also help identify a good deal easier when you can access what other properties are sold for comparable to the one you want to buy.

Keep in mind that this works mostly for single-family homes and duplexes. When you start getting into commercial buildings, you will use the CAP rate to compare one building to another (refer back to chapter four on calculating CAP rates). It is harder to find buildings that match each other in terms of size, location, age and recently sold within a year or less. You can use a couple of different websites that will help you find out how much properties in a certain area are being sold for or have sold for in the past. By the time you are old enough to read this, there will be many other websites or apps you can use than are available today.

Another key thing you will need to know about a property before you purchase it is the type of zoning that the property is in. This factor is truly important because, let's say, you decide to buy a single-family house with intentions to turn the basement into a legal suit. When you go to the city to get the permit needed to start the work, you find out that the house is currently in a zone where basement suites are not allowed. Your previous calculations on things like your cash flow and ROI will now be invalid, and now you have possibly made a bad investment.

I cannot stress how important it is for you to check the zoning information. If you buy a home with a basement suit and the area it's in isn't zoned for homes like that, then the city can come in any time and tell everyone except one family to vacate the premises. The city can also fine you, causing you to restructure your property to conform to the zone it is in. This situation can cost you thousands of dollars, not to mention the loss of rental income you anticipated.

If you are looking at buying commercial buildings, make sure that the building complies with all the environmental laws in place. If you don't do your due diligence for some reason and it turns out that the building is not in compliance, you will be on the hook to pay all the fines associated with each infraction.

You also want to get a survey done on the property before you buy it as well, as this will identify the actual property line and the land around it that you are buying. Sometimes the city can have what's called an easement on your property. An easement gives the city the right to use a certain part of your property for a specific reason without your permission. The city will most likely need to access a certain part of your land to work on things like power lines or other utilities that run under or above your property.

Your neighbor could also have an easement on a certain part of your property as well. They don't own it, but it gives them the ability to use that part of your land for a specific reason. For example, if they have to drive past your property to access the main road. This is why it is good to get a survey done on your property before purchasing it.

Another key thing you will need to know about a property is the types of things around or close to the property. The more stores, malls, restaurants, bars, and clubs you have around the area, the more foot traffic and vehicle traffic you will have. Additionally, this also means that more young professionals would like to live in this area, resulting in fewer vacancies. If the property you are purchasing isn't close to any of these things, then at least try to ensure that the property is close to some form of public transit. Ensuring proximity to public transit allows renters who cannot or don't want to live in a busy area, access to all amenities.

Keep in mind that big companies have to do a lot of research before deciding to go into any area and start building, leasing, or purchasing properties. So, if you see a lot of big company names around your property, then chances are they might know something that you might not yet. As I mentioned earlier, that's why it's important to walk around the area before purchasing.

The things listed above are just the minimum that every investor should know about each property before purchasing. Hopefully, when you are old enough to read this book, there will be a website or some form of software that you can use to get all this information. All you will have to do is type in the address of a location, and all this information will be available for you in a matter of seconds. If this website or software is still not available to you, this might be a good business idea for you to develop. To my knowledge, currently, there are websites you can go to that will tell you some of the information I listed above, but not all the information in one location.

CHAPTER 8

Passing Down Your Real-Estate Empire

Dear children, in this chapter, I will be going over how you can pass down your real estate empire to your children. There are a few different ways to accomplish this and keep in mind that each method has its pros and cons. It is critical that you do your research and hire the right people (lawyer and wealth manager) who deal with these types of transactions regularly to help you understand each method clearly.

In this chapter, I will be mainly forcing on the best way (in my opinion) to pass down your empire to your children, but I will also highlight a couple of other ways that you can achieve this same goal. It is truly important to clearly understand each method to select the best option that suits you and your family, as every family is different. There is no right or wrong way to do this, but there is the best way to do it. One particular method will be better suited to your family needs.

You will need to hire a wealth manager and lawyer to help guide you through this process because each country, state, province, and territory will have its own rules and regulations to follow. There is also the possibility that many of the current laws today might have changed by the time you read this book.

The first step you need to take to pass down your real estate empire to your children in the right way is to have a conversation with your family. Assuming that your children are adults, you will need to ask them if they even want to take over your real estate empire or not. Sometimes, parents' plans for their children turn out to be something that their child or children hate to do or are unable to do. It is important as a parent to understand this and develop an alternative way to leave the real estate empire to their children. On the other hand, if their child or children are enthusiastic about getting into real estate, then this would make leaving the real estate empire to them that much easier. If your children are under the age of 18 years, then it might be a good idea to have a trust set up for them that they can take over after they are old enough.

One of the first things you need to do, is to appoint a trustee. This will be the person in charge of the trust and it could be their mother or someone that you trust. The important thing to remember is to have a conversation with your family first. After the conversation, the next step would be to consult with a qualified wealth manager and lawyer. You will need to consult with them for them to guide you and your family through the process. I know that this conversation isn't an easy conversation to have with your family, but it is truly necessary.

It's also important to revise your plan regularly to account for any new changes that might have occurred from your last revision (like the purchase of a new property). You also want to make sure that when you leave your empire to your children, that they will truly enjoy their inheritance. You don't want it to become a burden to them and possibility their families.

One of the best ways (in my opinion), to leave your real estate empire to your children is by setting up what's called a revocable living trust. When you pass away, and you have assets, including real estate in your name, the government will take over your assets and use the courts to distribute them to your family members as they see fit (that is, unless you have a will). That is why you need to have a will. Your will serve as instructions for the court system to follow and divide your assets as instructed by your will. Your will can then allow your children to take over your real estate empire in their names legally.

The process between the time you pass away (with assets still in your name) until the court finally gives your children the assets you left for them is called the probate period (it also goes by other names). This process can take months and possibly cost your family members thousands of dollars. It can also become extremely stressful and create division between family members. This is where the revocable living trust comes into play, as it allows your family members to avoid the court process, hiring lawyers, and all other fees associated with the probate period. When you pass away, the last thing you want to do is have your family members run around looking for documentation, title deeds and hiring lawyers to help them through this process. It's easier for them if you were to retitle your assets into the trust. A revocable trust is created before you die, and it will allow your assets not to be taken over by the court system but instead, be taken over by someone you appoint (the trustee). Your trustee (normally a family member or family members, sometimes a lawyer) will then divide the assets accordingly amongst your children and spouse.

It's important to note that your assets must be retitled over to your revocable living trust before you pass away for them not to go through the probate process. Make sure to talk to your bank (or whoever loaned you the money to buy your assets) before you retitle the deed over to your trust. It's important to ensure that the retitling process doesn't trigger a due-on-sale clause (which I talked about in chapter six). Unfortunately, when you pass away and pass your real estate empire over to your children, they might have to pay an estate tax on the property (or properties) you have given them. Estate tax law differs by country, state, province, and territory, which is why it is important to do your research and hire a tax accountant who deals with estate taxes.

Some countries might not have estate taxes but will call it a capital gain tax instead. The good thing is that if your estate is below a certain value, you might not be required to pay taxes on it. On the other hand, if it is above the value stated by the law, you will only be required to pay taxes on the amount exceeding that set value. The value stated by the law differs by country, state, province, and territory, which is why it is important to do your research and hire a tax accountant who deals with estate taxes to help guide you through the process.

There are other ways to pass down your real estate empire to your children. You could give your empire to your children as a gift while you are still alive, or (if the country, state, province, or territory that you have your assets in allows you) you can do what is called a Transfer on Death deed. It's also important to note that each of those options has its own tax and legal implications. Each family is different, so what might work for one family might not be ideal for another. That is why it is important to consult with a lawyer and tax accountant to help you with this process. Make sure you regularly communicate with your spouse as well about these things. It is not a fun conversation to have, but it's necessary, as I said earlier.

CHAPTER 9

▬▬▬▬▬

Words of Wisdom

Dear children, I hope this book helped you see the power of generational wealth and showed you some ways of achieving it. I hope that this empowers you to take action and understand that you can do anything you want to do in this world. Make sure to research because each country, state, and province might have different rules and regulations, understand the risks, and have a step-by-step process of how you will achieve your goals. Ensure that you hire accountants and lawyers who regularly deal with real estate to help you with this process. The real estate agent, property manager, mortgage broker, and the person doing your inspections all have to have years of experience dealing with the type of property you want to acquire.

This book is meant to open up your eyes to the possibilities of what real estate can do for you and your family. Each chapter can be broken down and made into its own book. I am sure that they are plenty of books out there about those very topics. I encourage you to read them and find out as much as you can about the real estate business. Remember to make sure your credit is in good standing, select a cash-flowing property, hire the right team, and have a plan on how you will pass down your empire to your children. Also, remember to get the right type of insurance, do extensive research on each property you are going to purchase, including that market that it is located in.

It will be Jayden's (our firstborn child) birthday soon, and he will be turning one year old. By the time he reads this book, many things will have changed in the real estate industry, as it always has. You might be living in a different country that will have different rules and regulations. This possibility is why I am always repeating the fact that you need to do your research a lot in this book. Use this book as your guide. The principles have remained constant over the past decades, it's mainly the processes that have changed.

All the best with whatever path you decide to follow, and remember to put God first. Always remember that your mother and I love you so much. You have already made us so proud.

Manufactured by Amazon.ca
Bolton, ON